KIDS PROGRAMMING 1

Written by:
Kensho Koyama &
Mindaugas Ramanauskis

Chestnut Tree
LEARNING©

Written by: Kensho Koyama & Mindaugas Ramanauskis

INDEX

ATTENTION!!

Before using this textbook, please access all lesson materials using the link below

- Unit 1-10 Warm-ups
- Student lesson projects
- Teacher lesson projects (completed)

UNIT 1: Basketball

1.

basketball

2.

gym

3.

net

Basketball Chant

Bounce, bounce, the **basketball**
at the **gym play basketball**
shoot the ball in the **net**
how many baskets can you get? 1, 2, 3, 4, 5

WORDBANK	
basketball	bounce
gym	play
net	shoot

UNIT 1: Basketball

1.

Yes I did it!

2.

Yes I did it!

3.

Yes I did it!

Extra Programming

Yes I did it!

UNIT 1: Basketball

1

3

2

Color:

UNIT 1: Basketball

Maze

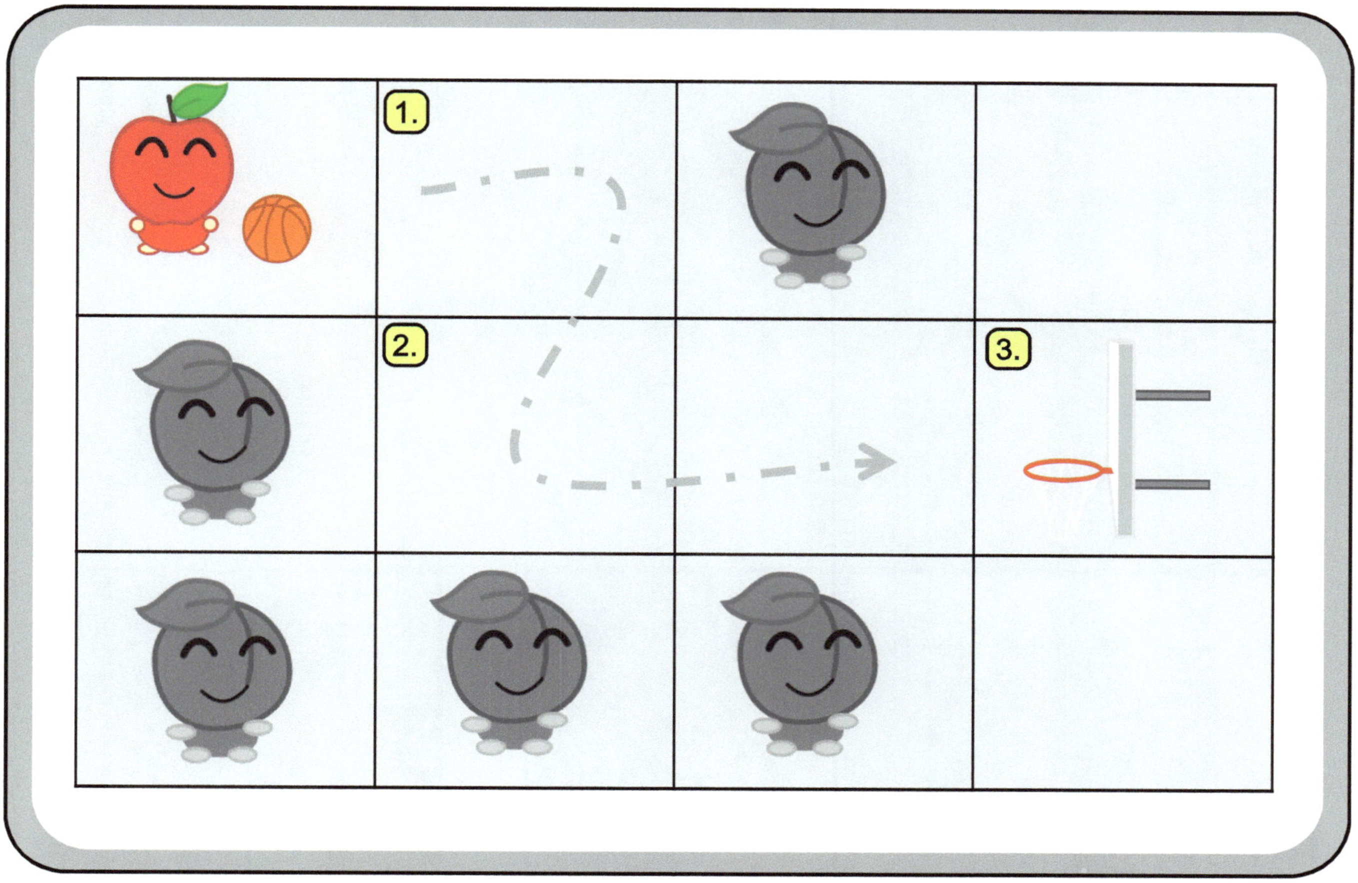

Maze code

1.

2.

3.

UNIT 2: Bowling

1.

bowling ball

2.

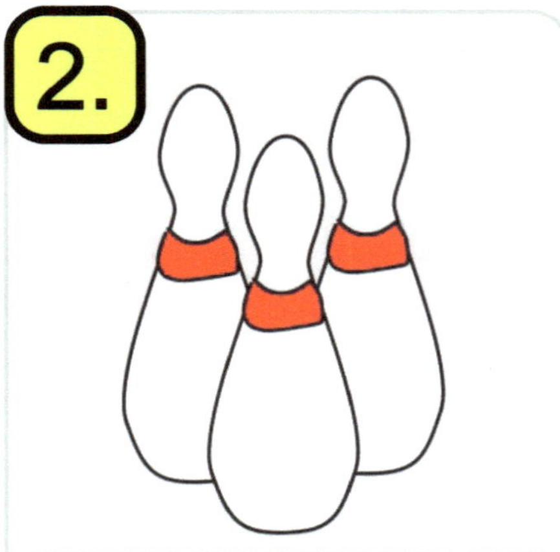

pins

3.

strike

Bowling Chant

Pick up a **bowling ball**, and hold it in your hands, give it a **roll**, **hit** down all the **pins**,
1,2,3,4,5,6,7,8,9,10,
get a **strike** and win.

Can you go bowling?

WORDBANK	
bowling ball	roll
pins	hit
strike	get

UNIT 2: Bowling

1.

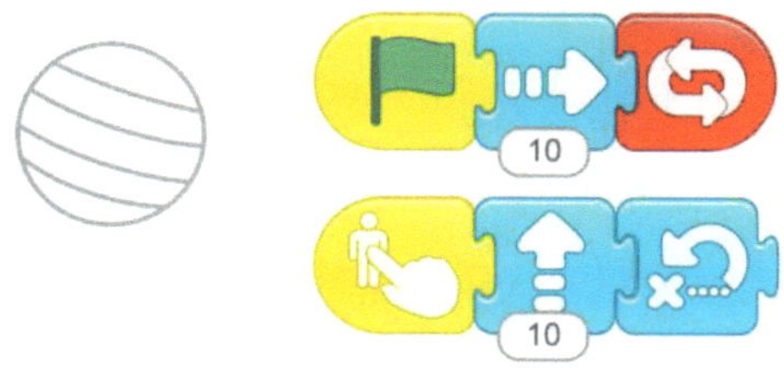

Yes I did it!

2.

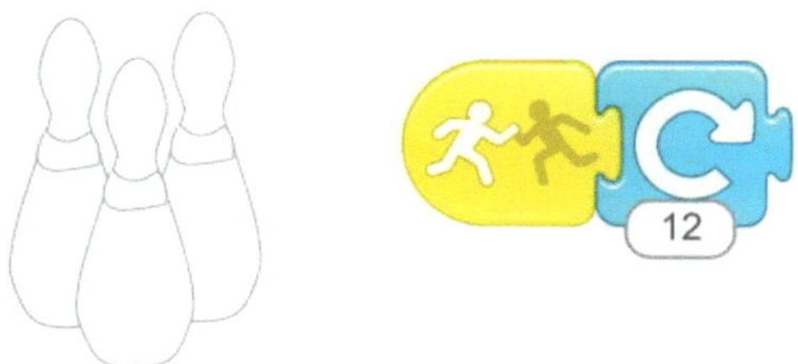

Yes I did it!

3.

Yes I did it!

Extra Programming

Yes I did it!

UNIT 2: Bowling

Connect:

6

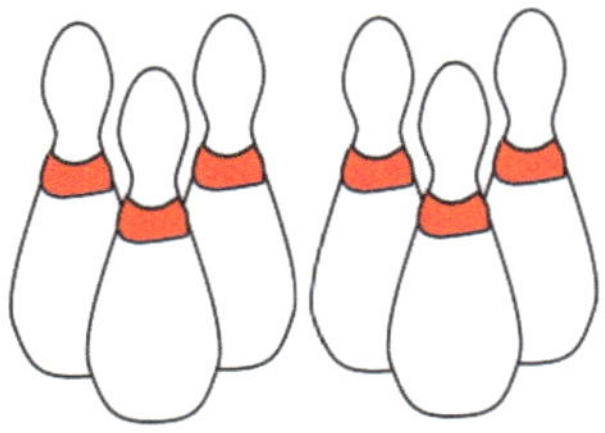

3

2

Count: 1 - 10

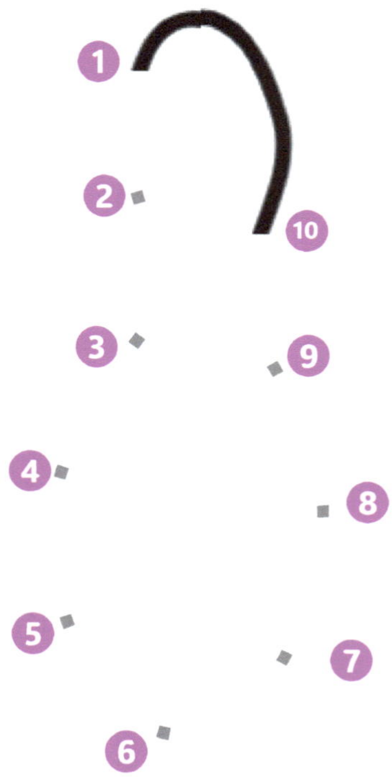

UNIT 2: Bowling

Maze:

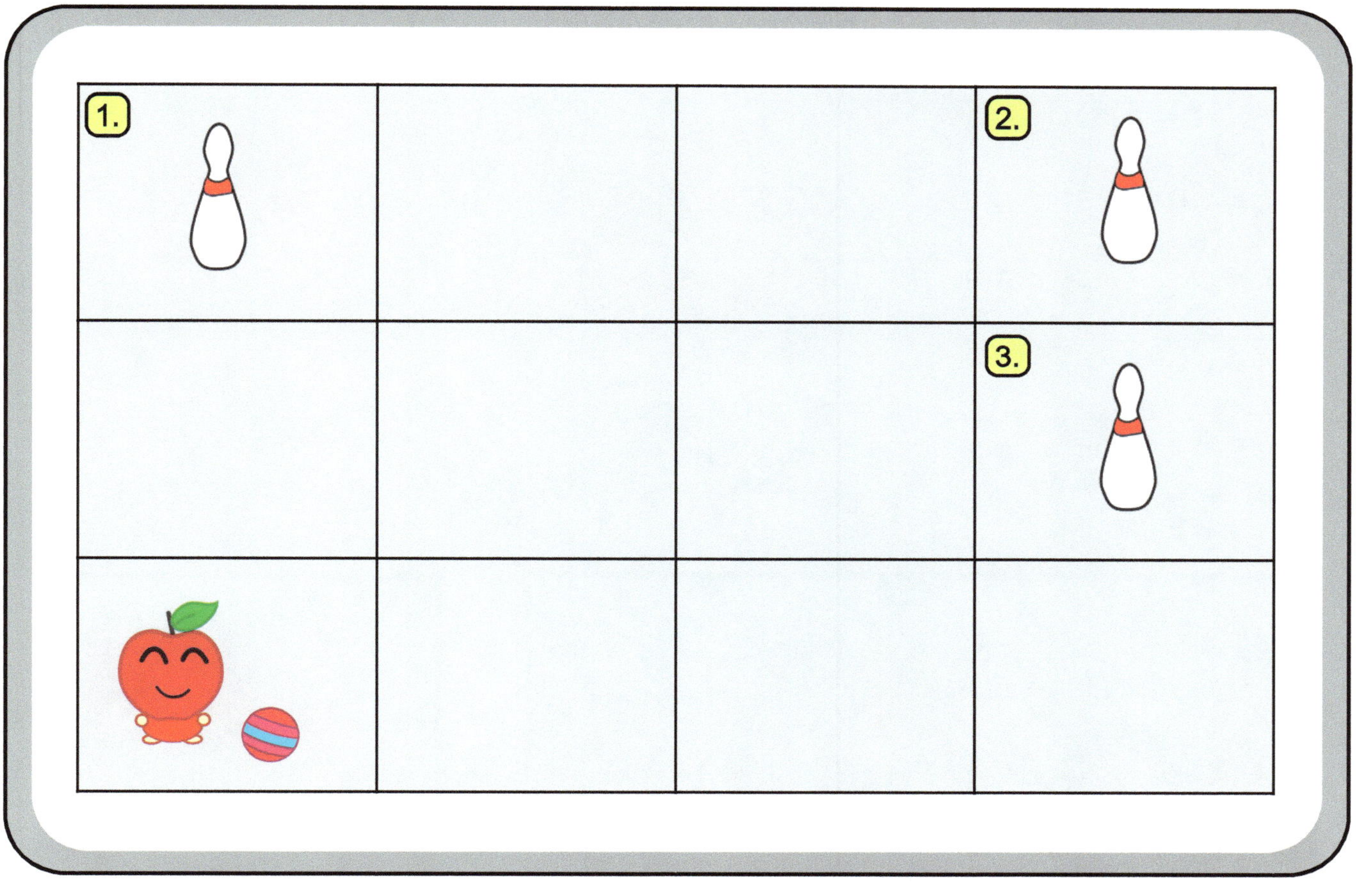

Maze code:

1.

2.

3.

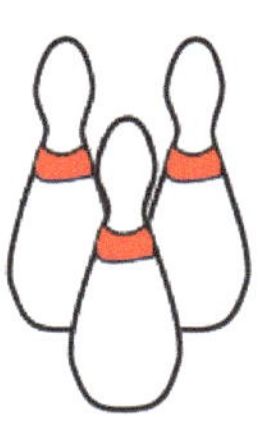

UNIT 3: Firefighters

1.

fire

2.

firefighters

3.

water

Fire Fighter Chant

Firefighters coming, driving on the way,
got the fire hose, with **water** to **spray**,
spray the **fire out**, spray the **fire out**, after
that we'll all go home for the day

Can you fight a fire?

WORDBANK	
fire	out
firefighters	coming
water	spray

UNIT 3: Fire Fighters

1.

Yes I did it!

2.

Yes I did it!

3.

Yes I did it!

Extra Programming

Yes I did it!

UNIT 3: Fire Fighters

Connect:

Find the code:

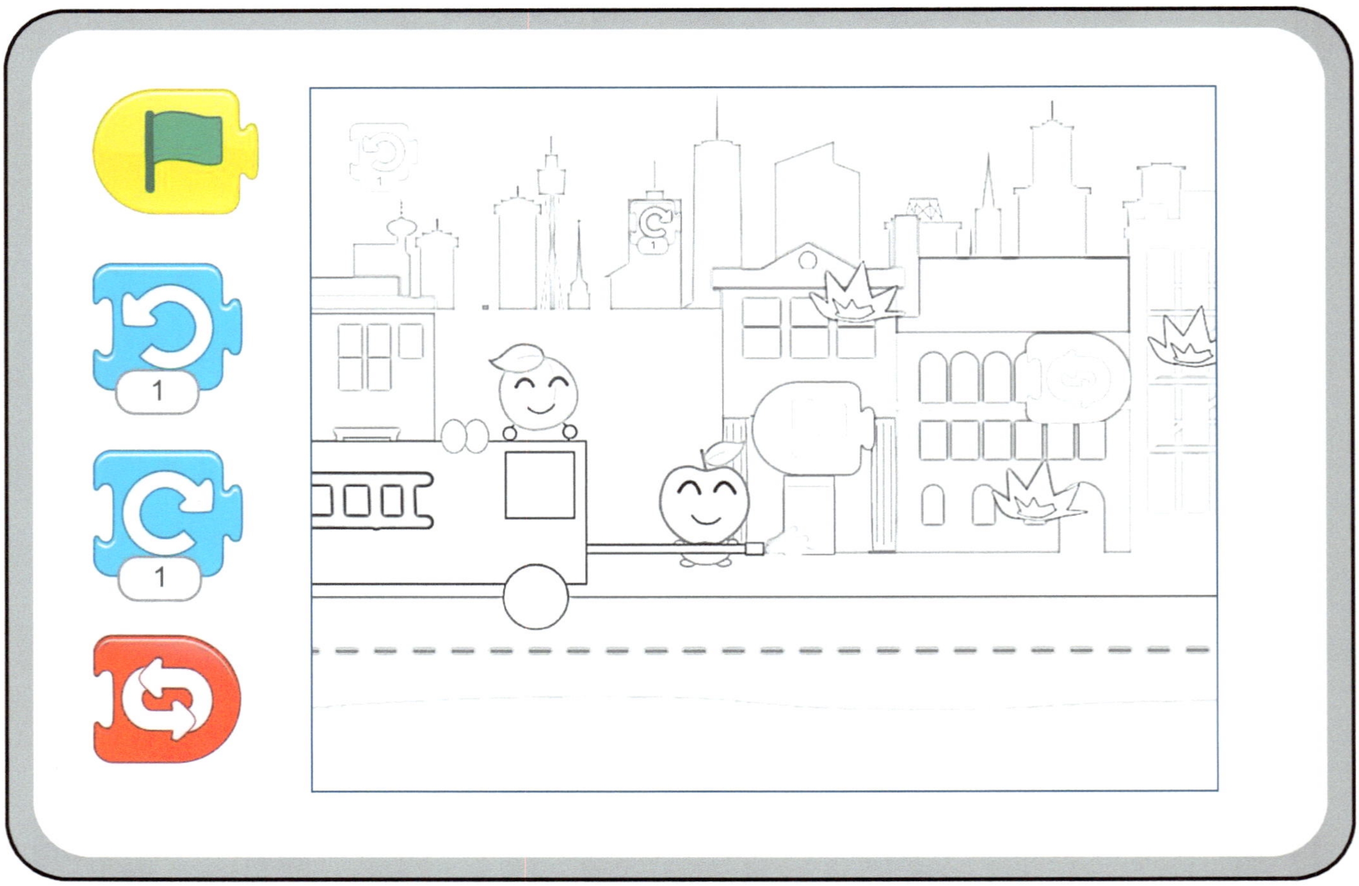

UNIT 3: Fire Fighters

Maze:

Maze code:

1.

2.

3.

UNIT 4: Fire Fighters 2

1.

fire truck

2.

cat

3.

tree

Fire Fighters 2 Chant

Fire fighters come, in their **firetruck**

to help the **cat**, who got stuck

climb the ladder, up the **tree**

to help the **cat**, to get free

Can you save a cat?

WORDBANK	
firetruck	sound
cat	meow
tree	climb

UNIT 4: Fire Fighters 2

1.

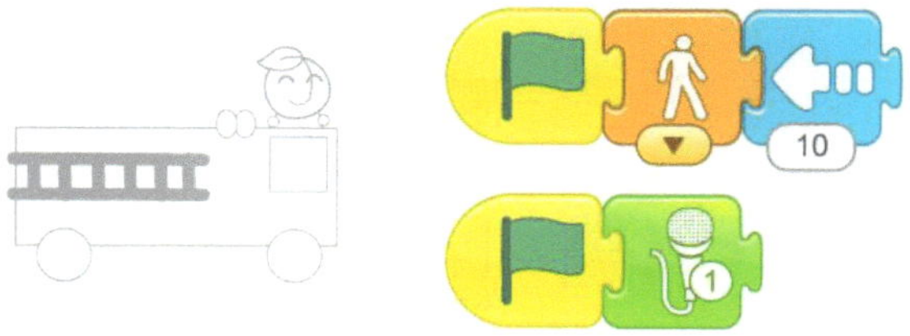

Yes I did it!

2.

Yes I did it!

3.

Yes I did it!

Extra Programming

Yes I did it!

UNIT 4: Fire Fighters 2

Connect:

4

3

2

Maze:

UNIT 4: Fire Fighters 2

Write:

1 1 1

2 2 2

3 3 3

4 4 4

Draw a fire:

UNIT 5: Car Race

1.

car

2.

road

3.

finish line

Race Car Chant

Race my **car** out on the **road**,
cross the **finish line**, ready, set, go,
drive drive fast, in my **car**, **drive drive**
fast, in my **car, drive drive** fast, in my **car!**

WORDBANK	
car	drive
road	race
finish line	cross

UNIT 5: Car Race

1.

Yes I did it!

2.

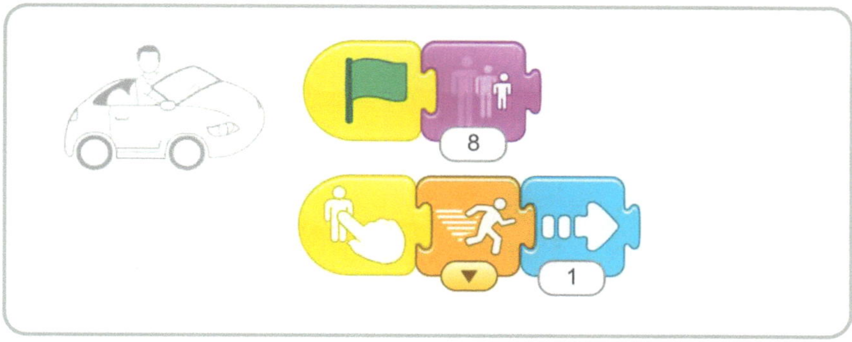

Yes I did it!

3.

Yes I did it!

Extra Programming

Yes I did it!

UNIT 5: Car Race

Connect:

1

2

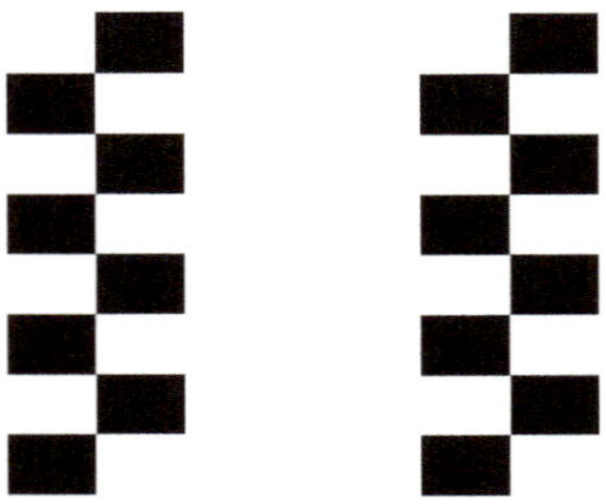

5

Maze:

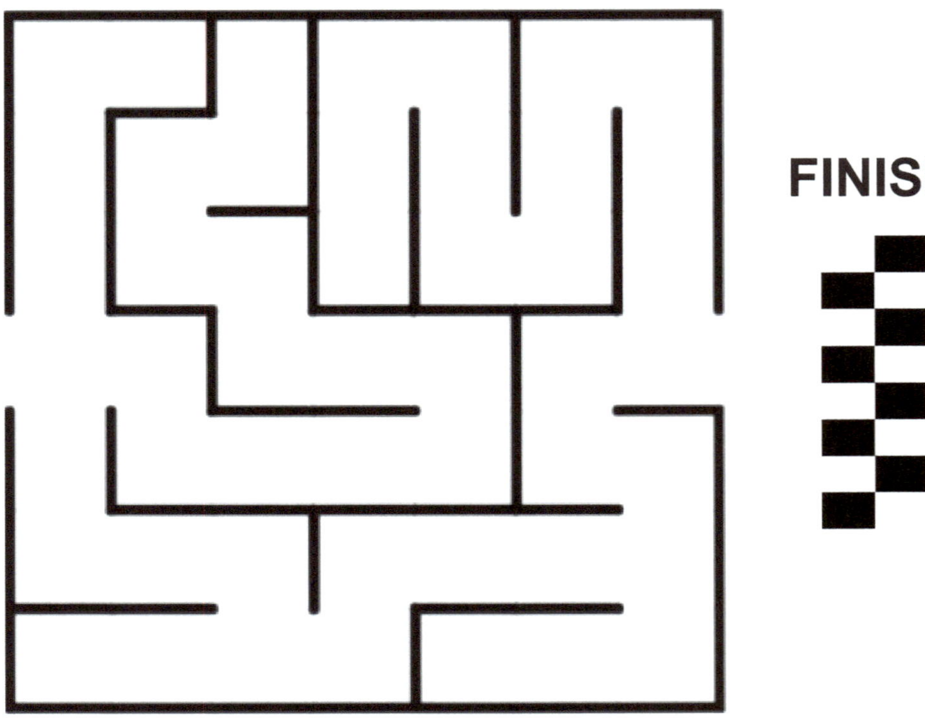

UNIT 5: Car Race

Code Search:

Color:

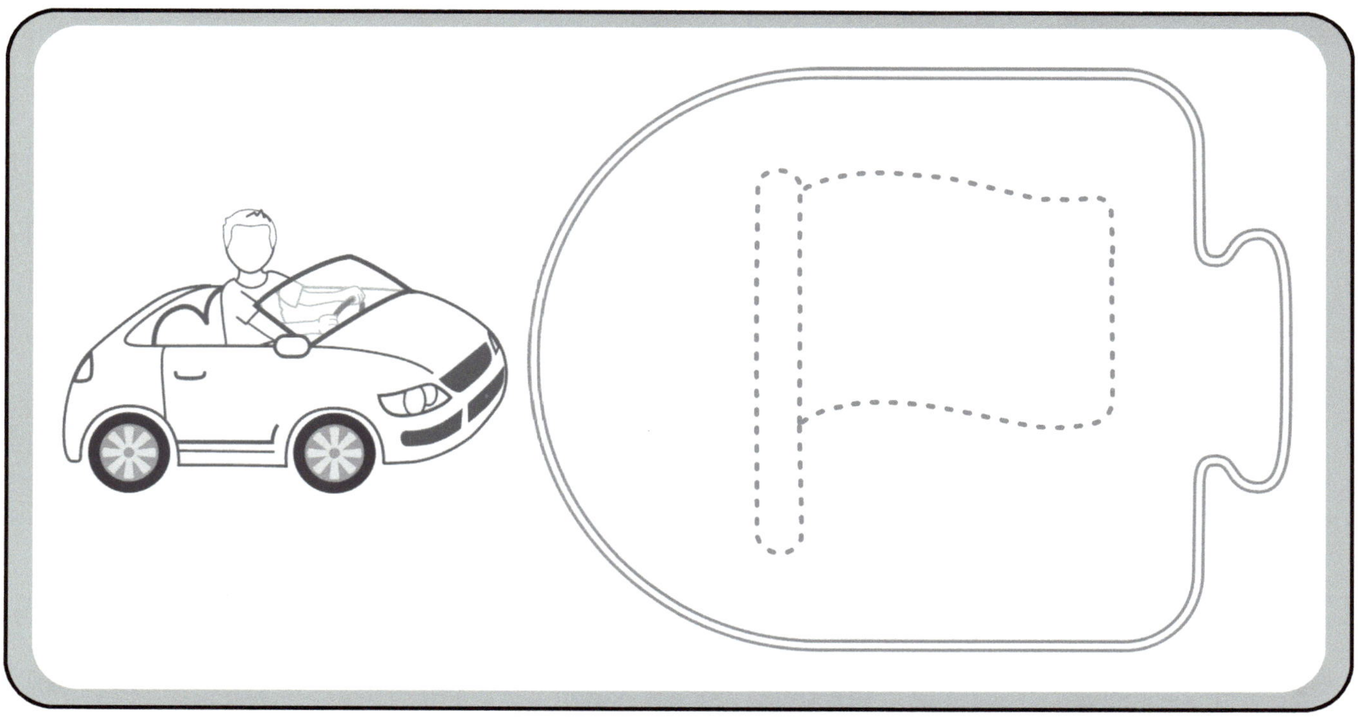

UNIT 6: Soccer

1.

player

2.

soccer ball

3.

goal

Soccer Chant

Kick the **soccer ball, kick, kick, kick**

Run to the **soccer ball, run, run, run**

Pass the soccer ball **pass, pass, pass**

Shoot the soccer ball. Yay I scored a **goal**!

WORDBANK	
player	run
soccer ball	kick
goal	scored

UNIT 6: Soccer

1.

Yes I
did it!

2.

Yes I
did it!

3.

Yes I
did it!

Extra Programming

Yes I
did it!

UNIT 6: Soccer

Connect:

6

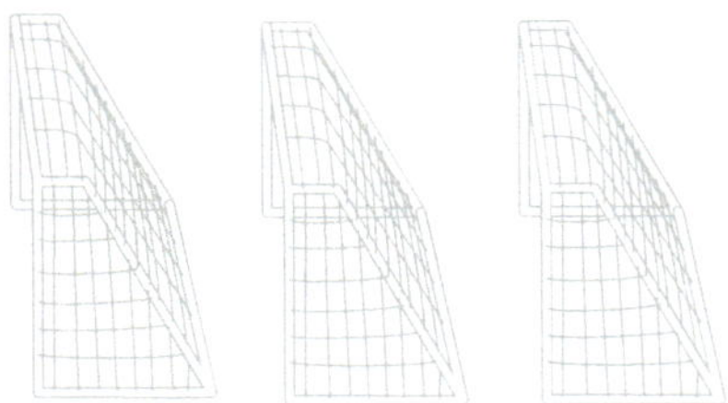

8

3

Count 1-10:

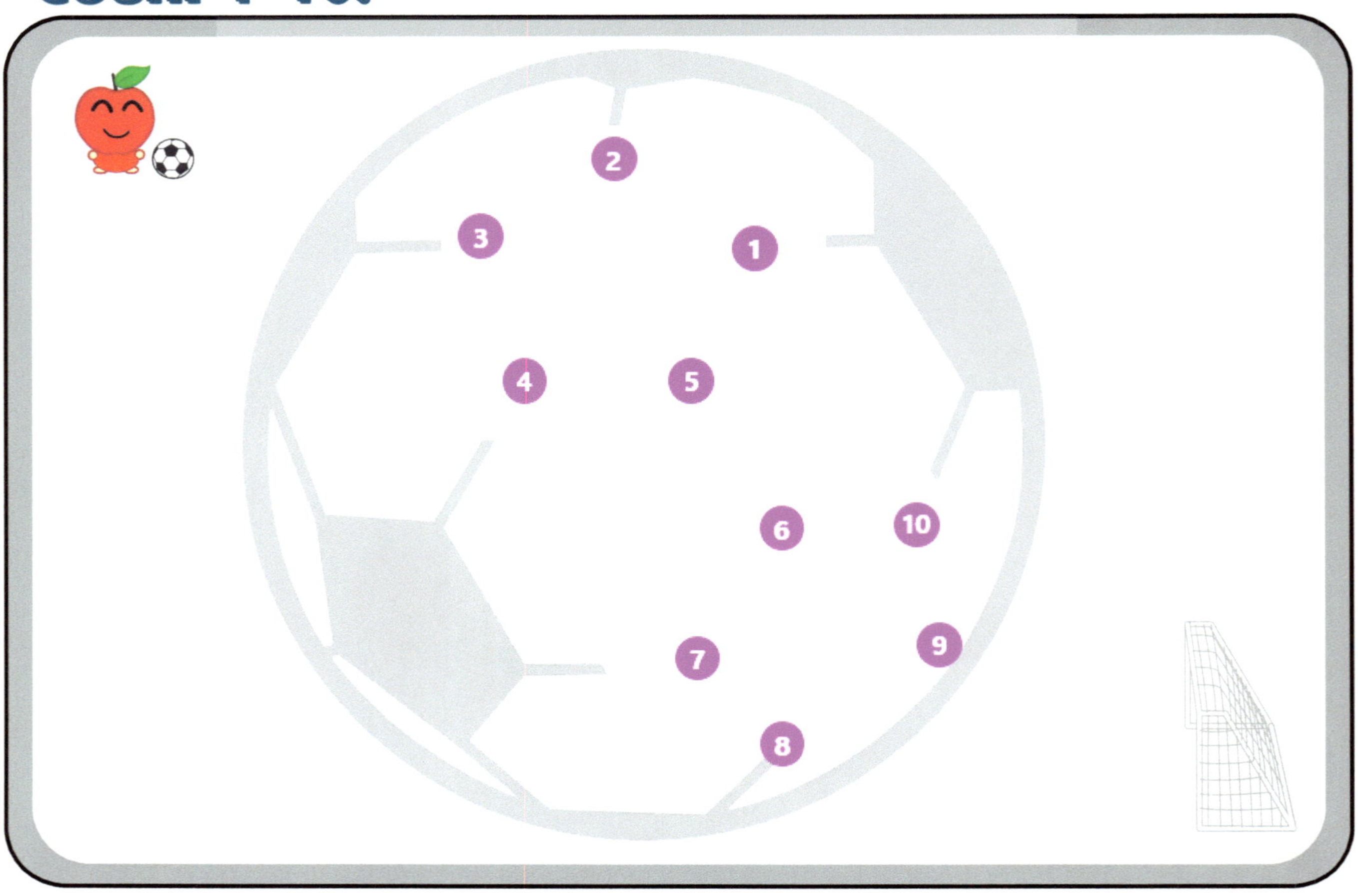

UNIT 6: Soccer

Maze:

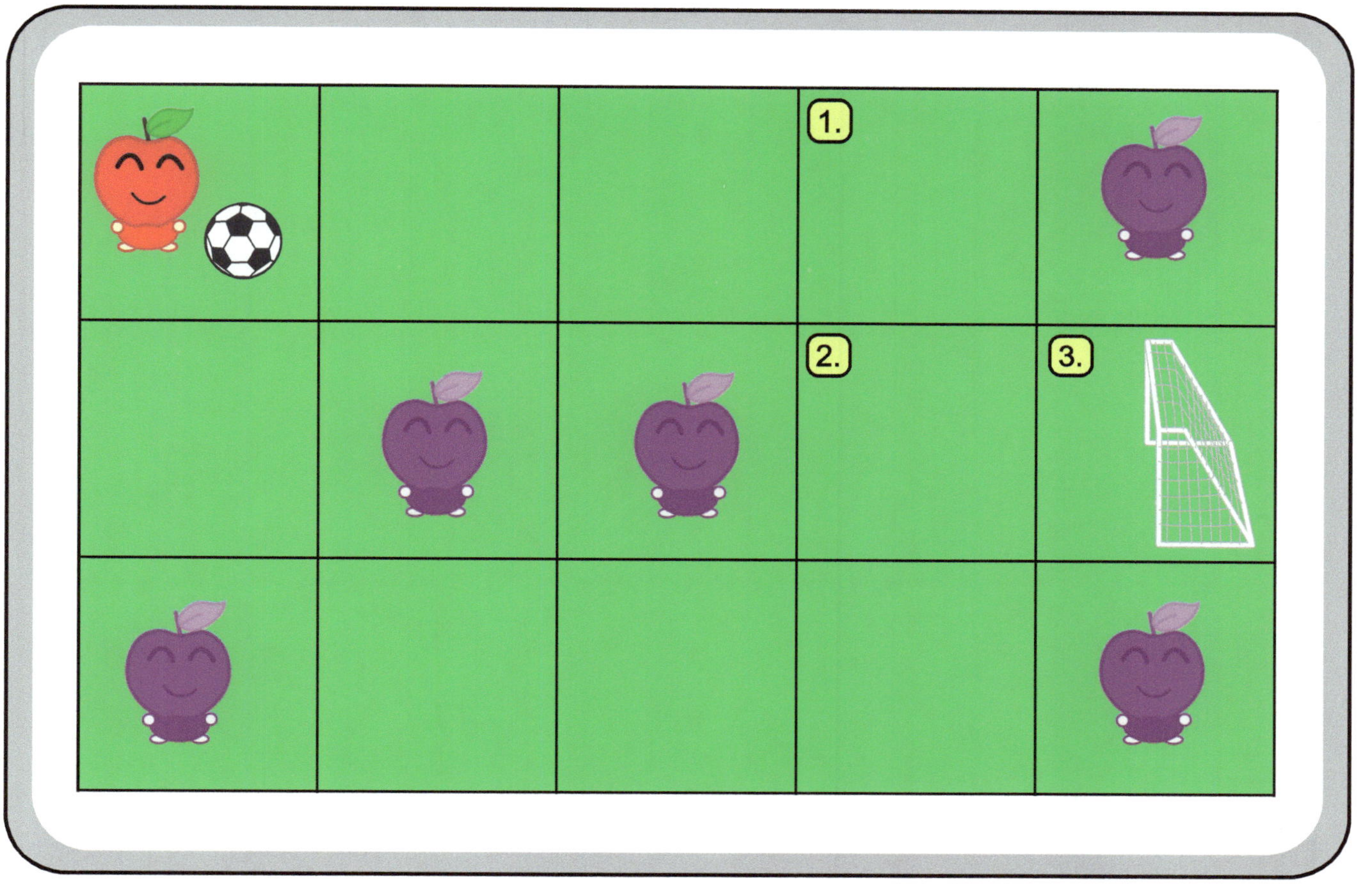

Maze code:

1.

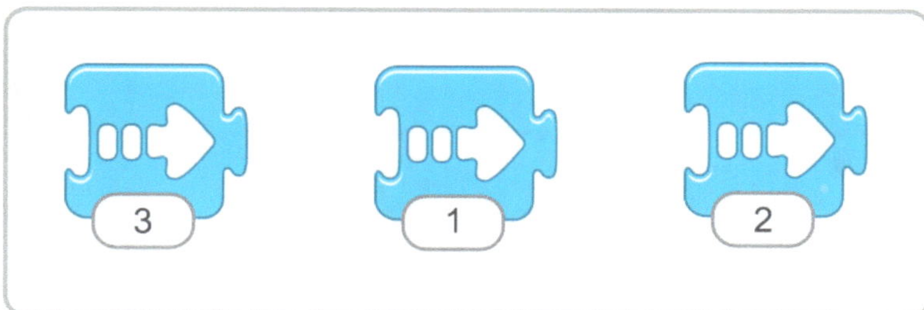

2.

3.

UNIT 7: Design

1.

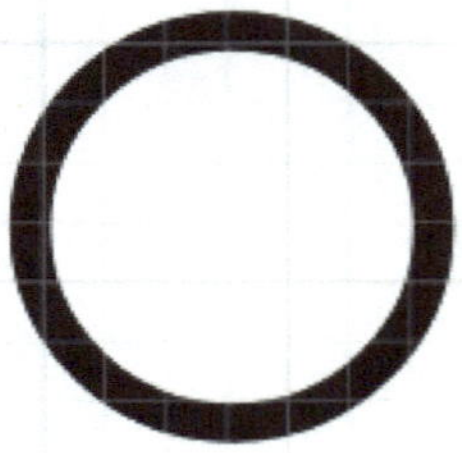

circle

2.

paint bucket

3.

character

Design Chant

Close, close, close your eyes

what colors can you see?

I can see **red, purple, yellow,**

orange, blue and **green**.

Can you draw a caterpillar?

WORDBANK	
red	purple
blue	orange
yellow	green

UNIT 7: Design

1.

Yes I did it!

2.

Yes I did it!

3.

1)

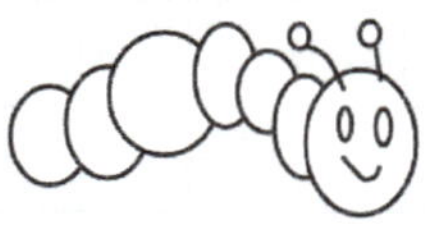

2)

Yes I did it!

Extra Programming

Yes I did it!

UNIT 7: Design

Connect:

7

4

3

Draw:

UNIT 7: Design

Circle:

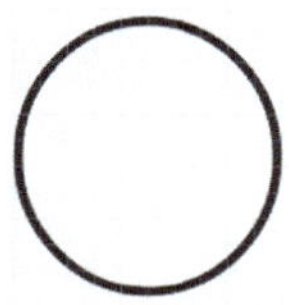

 or 

 or 

 or 

Draw:

UNIT 8: Caterpillar

1.

caterpillar

2.

apple

3.

big caterpillar

Caterpillar Chant

The **caterpillar crawls** wow, wow, wow
eating fruit, look at him now ♫
he **bites** the **apple**, munch, munch, munch
growing big, with every crunch

Can you feed a caterpillar?

WORDBANK	
caterpillar	crawls
apple	bites
big	growing

UNIT 8: Caterpillar

1.

Yes I did it!

2.

Yes I did it!

3.

Yes I did it!

Extra Programming

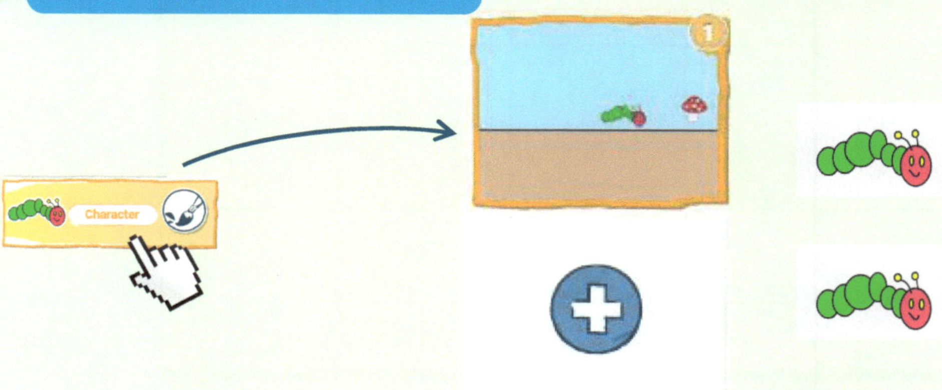

Yes I did it!

UNIT 8: Caterpillar

Connect:

6

11

9

Color and Complete:

Eat the peaches

UNIT 8: Caterpillar

Write:

5 5 5

6 6 6

7 7 7

8 8 8

Color:

UNIT 9: Zoo Animals

1.

jungle

2.

hello

3.

animals

Zoo Animals Chant

In the **jungle** what a **show**,
all the **animals say hello**,
hear, hear, all the **animals**,
hear hear the **animals** (2x), all **say hello**.

Can you make animal sounds?

WORDBANK	
jungle	show
hello	say
animals	hear

Yes I can!

UNIT 9: Zoo Animals

1.

Yes I did it!

2.

Yes I did it!

3.

Yes I did it!

Extra Programming

Yes I did it!

UNIT 9: Zoo Animals

Connect:

5

12

2

Find the Code:

UNIT 9: Zoo Animals

Maze:

Maze code:

1.

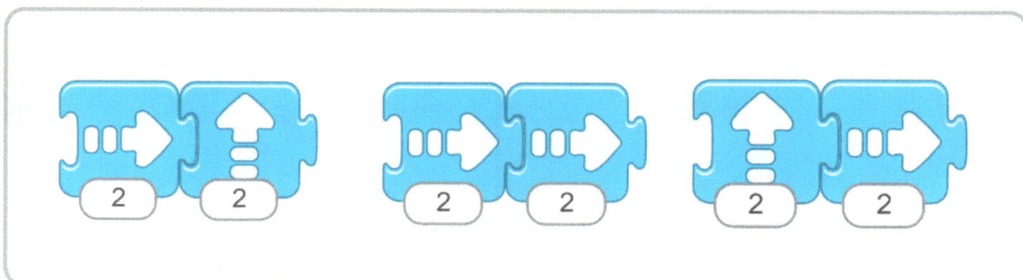

2.

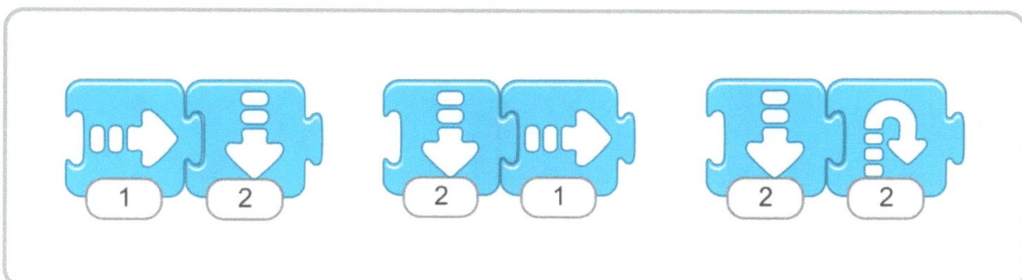

3.

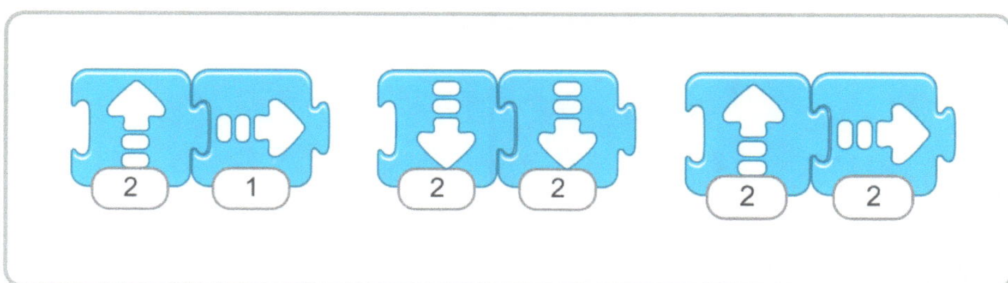

UNIT 10: Archery

1.

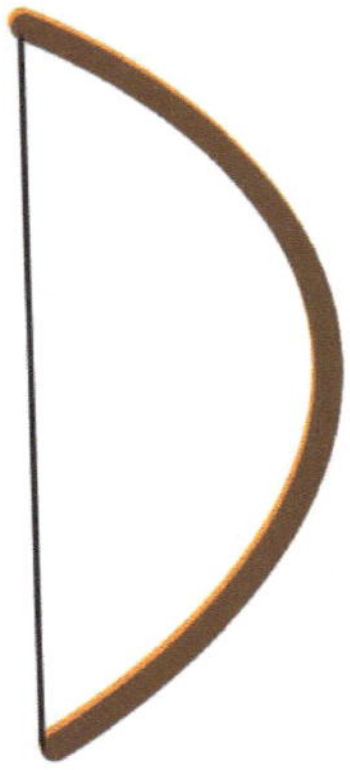

bow

2.

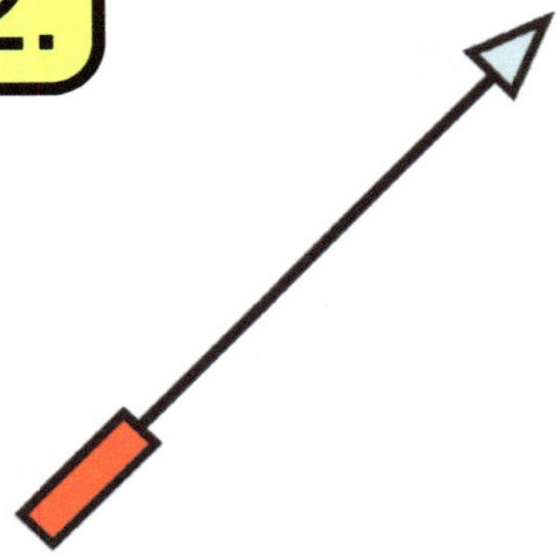

arrow

3.

archery

Archery Chant

Pull the **bow**,

aim the **arrow**,

take your **shot**,

archery fun, we like it a lot!

WORDBANK	
bow	pull
arrow	aim
archery	shot

UNIT 10: Archery

1.

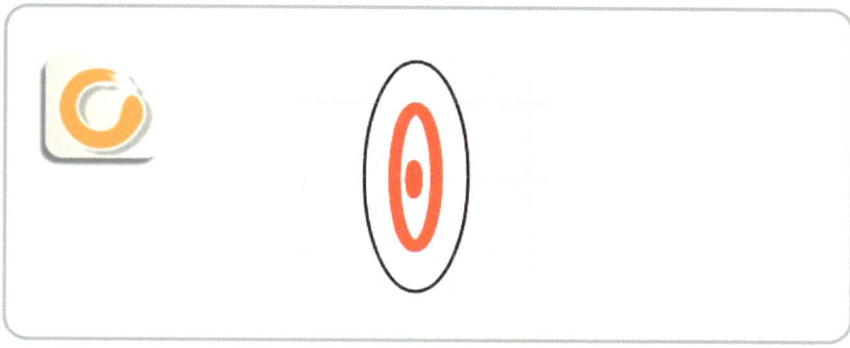

Yes I did it!

2.

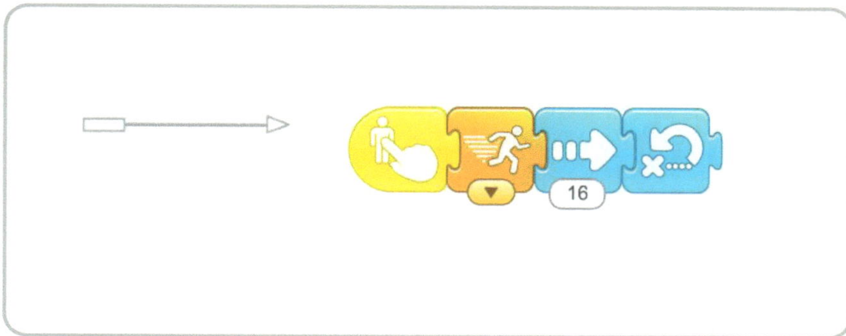

Yes I did it!

3.

Yes I did it!

Extra Programming

Yes I did it!

UNIT 10: Archery

Connect:

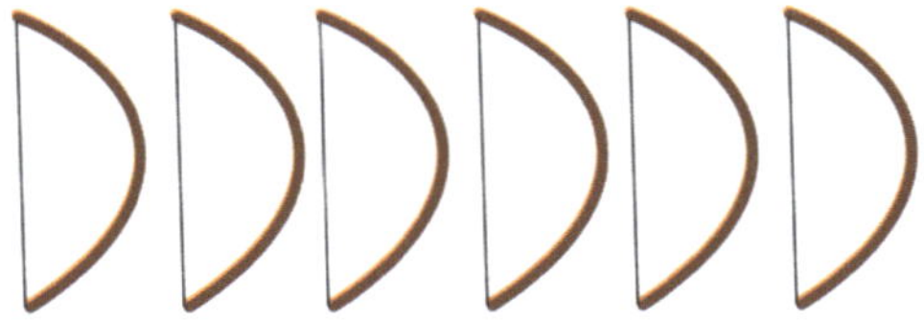

6

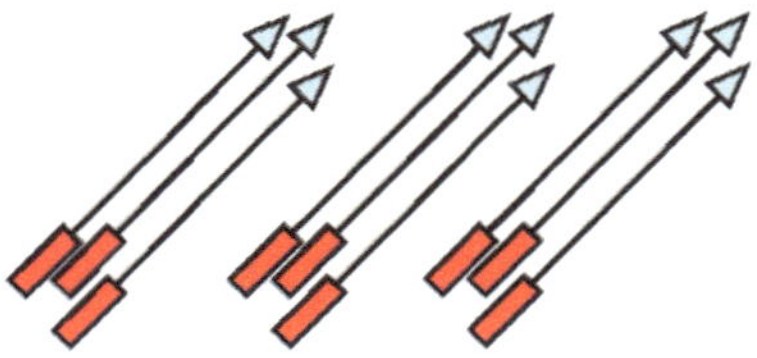

9

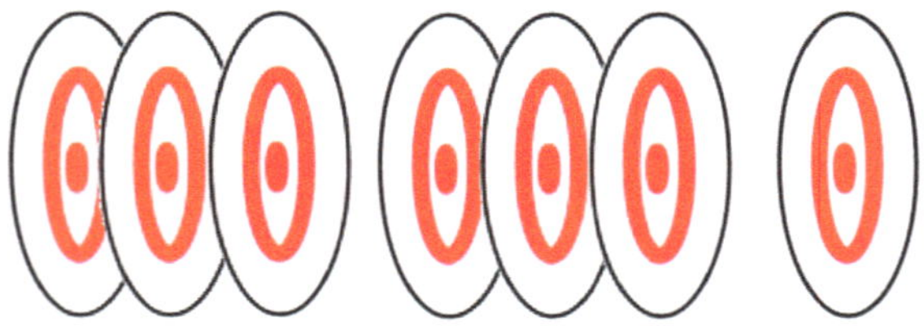

7

Maze:

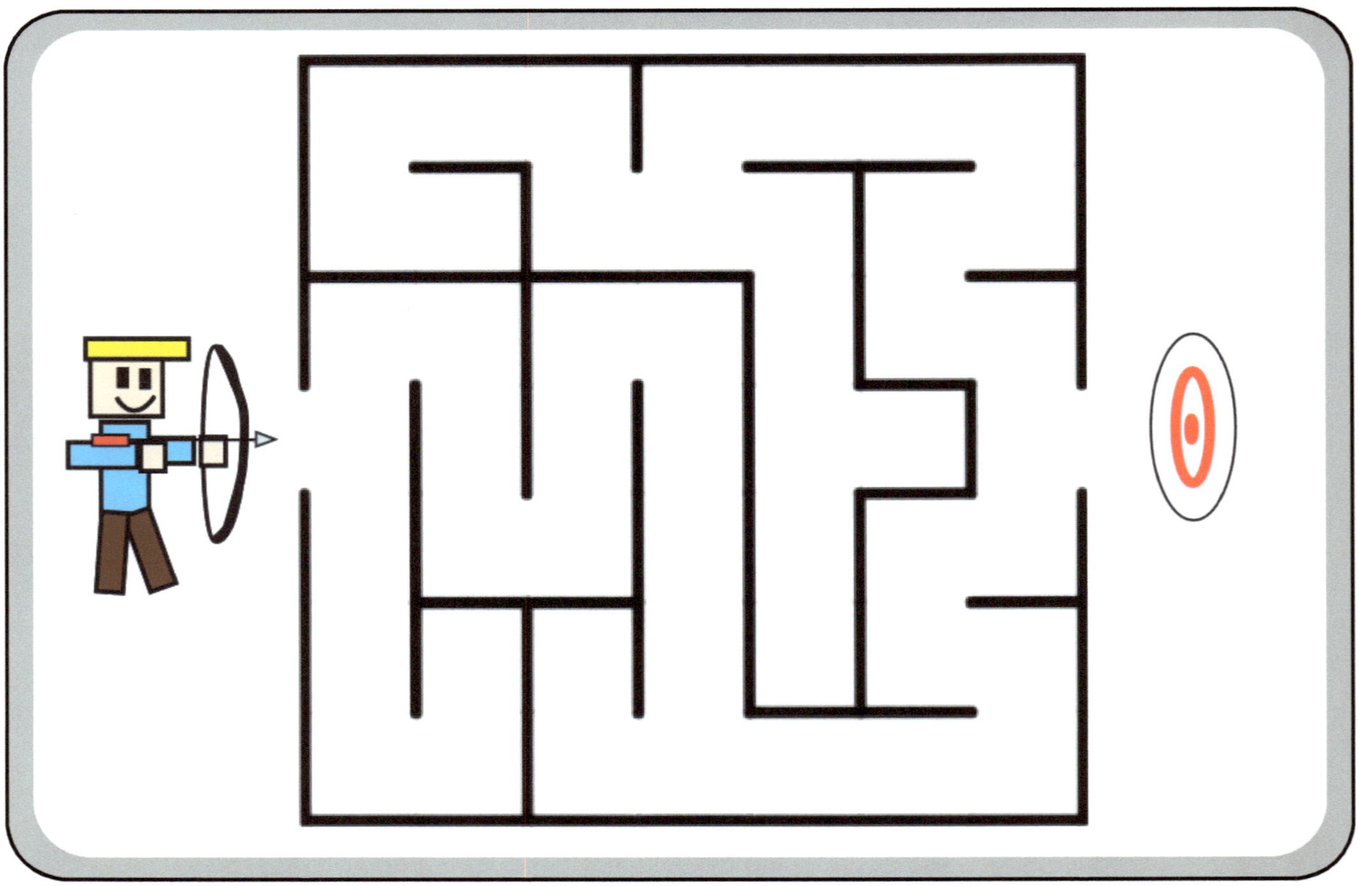

UNIT 10: Archery

Code Search:

Color:

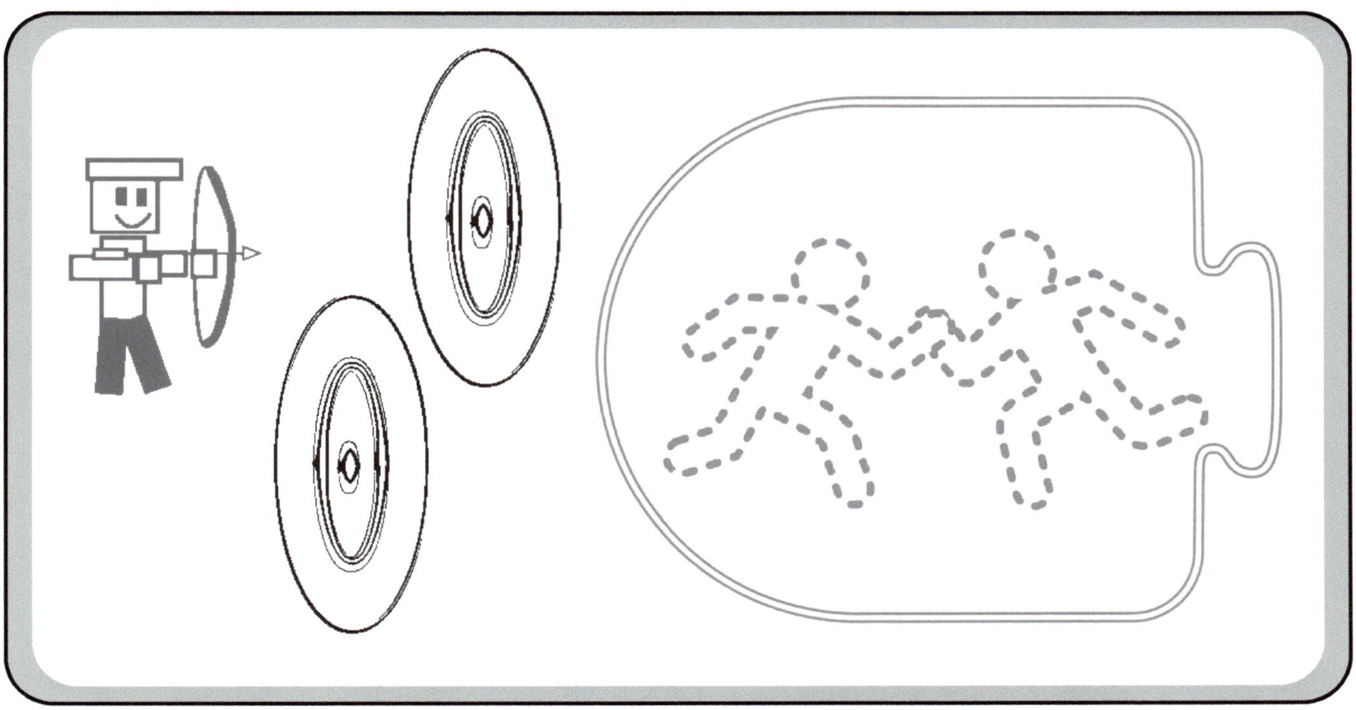

Start on green flag

Start on tap

Start on bump

Start on message

Send a message

Move forward

Move back

Move up

Move down

Turn right

Turn left

End

Repeat forever

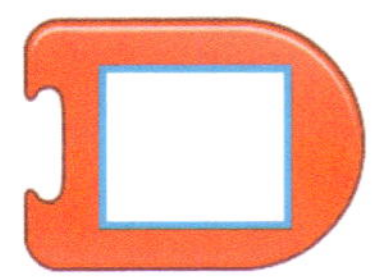

Go to page

Hop

Go home

Say

Grow

Shrink

Reset size

Hide

Show

Play

Wait

Stop

Set speed

repeat

CHESTNUT TREE
LEARNING©

Written by: Kensho Koyama & Mindaugas Ramanauskis

www.ingramcontent.com/pod-product-compliance
Lightning Source LLC
Chambersburg PA
CBHW041324210926
51847CB00003B/43
9784991443107